Spending Money

by Natalie M. Rosinsky

Content Adviser: Jaclyn B. H. Finstad, New Ulm, Minnesota;
M.B.A., University of Findlay, Ohio

Reading Adviser: Dr. Alexa Sandmann, Professor of Literacy,
The Universty of Toledo; Member, International Reading Association

Let's See Library
Compass Point Books
Minneapolis, Minnesota

Compass Point Books
3109 West 50th Street, #115
Minneapolis, MN 55410

Visit Compass Point Books on the Internet at *www.compasspointbooks.com* or e-mail your request to *custserv@compasspointbooks.com*

On the cover: A mother and daughter buy fruit at a market.

Photographs ©: Elizabeth Hathon/Corbis, cover; Corbis, 4; AFP/Corbis, 6; D. Yeske/Visuals Unlimited, 8; Mug Shots/Corbis, 10; Claro Cortes IV/Reuters/Hulton/Archive by Getty Images, 12; Ed Bock/Corbis, 14; Jeff Greenberg/Visuals Unlimited, 16; Skjold Photographs, 18; Paul Barton/Corbis, 20; John Cross/The Free Press, 24.

Editor: Catherine Neitge
Photo Researcher: Svetlana Zhurkina
Designers: Melissa Voda/Jaime Martens

Library of Congress Cataloging-in-Publication Data
Rosinsky, Natalie M. (Natalie Myra)
Spending money / by Natalie M. Rosinsky.
p. cm. — (Let's see library. Economics) (Let's see library)
Includes bibliographical references and index.
ISBN 0-7565-0485-6
1. Consumption (Economics)—Juvenile literature. [1. Money. 2. Finance, Personal.] I. Title. II. Series. III. Series: Let's see library
HC79.C6R67 2004
332.024--dc21 2002156026

Table of Contents

NOTE: In this book, words that are defined in the glossary are in **bold** *the first time they appear in the text.*

Why Do People Spend Money?

Your feet have grown again! You *need* new shoes. When you shop, will you buy cheap ones? Or will you *want* fancy ones that cost more? **Consumers** spend money on things they need. They also spend money on things they just want.

Sometimes, people **donate** money to help others. Some families donate regularly to **charity.** People also regularly pay **taxes.** The government uses this money for schools, roads, and other important things. A few people waste their money. They may **gamble** or buy many things they do not need.

◄ *Friends shop together to buy clothes they need and want.*

How Do People Plan Their Spending?

People, businesses, and governments all plan their spending. They do not want to run out of money! This kind of plan is called a **budget.**

First, they choose a time period. They list their regular **income** during this time. Next, they list their **expenses** during the same time. What will they *need* to spend money on? What are things they just *want?*

They subtract needed expenses from income. Any remaining money may be saved or spent on less important things. A budget helps people use money wisely.

◄ *Secretary of State Colin Powell explains the State Department budget to Congress.*

SAFETY FIRST!
MAGNA

How Can You Budget Your Own Money?

Will you have enough money next week? Plan ahead with a budget. Add up your regular income. Include **allowance** and money you regularly earn. Don't count birthday money before you get it! Now, add up your needed expenses. Do you pay for school lunch? Do you donate a dollar every week? Subtract such expenses from your income.

Is enough money left to see a movie? Will you be able to save for that new bike? Perhaps you will want to do extra chores to earn more.

◀ *A girl checks the price of a new bike.*

Thank You for
shopping Big Y.
Please let us know how
we can serve you better

What Are Other Ways to Spend Wisely?

Smart shoppers compare prices. Is one store selling your new shoes more cheaply than another? Look in several stores before you buy. Wise consumers also wait for sales and use coupons. These are ways to "stretch" your dollars!

If your new shoes tear, will the store give you another pair? Has the shoe factory promised to fix such problems? Some things come with a warranty like this. Before spending money, wise consumers ask about warranties. Smart shoppers also understand advertising.

◀ *Using coupons can save money at the grocery store.*

中国联通
CHINA UNICOM
CDMA
热卖场

What Should You Know About Advertising?

Laws require stores and companies to be honest. They must not lie about what they sell or make or do. Some advertising, though, fools consumers. You have to be careful about those ads.

Some other ads may feature a famous person. Will you choose new shoes because a star ball player wears them? Another ad shows many happy kids wearing a different kind of shoe. Will you buy these, instead? Some advertising sells things through bright colors, fun music, or clever pictures.

These kinds of advertising often reach consumers through their feelings, not their good sense.

◄ *A woman walks by a huge advertisement for a Chinese telephone service that features Houston Rockets basketball star Yao Ming.*

How Do People Borrow Money to Spend?

Buying a home costs a lot! Many people borrow money from a bank for this expense.

Each month, they pay back part of this **loan.** They also pay extra money. This money is the **interest** the bank charges. Interest is what a bank earns from a loan. Different loans may have different interest amounts, or rates.

Home loans are called mortgages. People use bank loans for other large expenses, too. These include buying a car and paying for college. Before lending such big sums, a bank is very careful. It looks closely at the borrower's income and work record.

◀ *A woman happily receives the keys to her new car. People often borrow money for such purchases.*

PULSAR

How Do People Use Credit Cards to Spend?

Stores and banks often offer **credit cards** to consumers. Even people with small incomes can easily get credit cards. Some teenagers even have their own credit cards!

Different cards may have different spending limits. These plastic cards work like loans. Cardholders make monthly payments on the amount they have spent. Interest is charged each month that the bill is not fully paid. Different cards may have different interest rates.

People sometimes spend foolishly with credit cards. With added interest, they pay more for the things they buy. Some people go into **debt** because of this.

◄ *A teenager uses her credit card to buy a watch.*

What Can People Do to Limit Spending?

Some people believe consumers buy too much. They think spending less would help our world. There would be less waste. Time now spent shopping could be better used.

Consumers have choices. So do you! Do you *need* or just *want* to buy something? Perhaps you could make that birthday present for your friend. Instead of spending money on a movie, you might spend time in a park. Perhaps you could borrow, not buy, a bike. Instead of buying a game, maybe you could trade games with a friend.

◀ *A boy works on an art project to give as a gift.*

How Will People Spend Money in the Future?

More and more people will spend **electronic money.** Already, some people use plastic **debit cards** instead of cash. Some "smart" credit and debit cards keep track of a person's spending. Cards soon will hold even more facts about someone's finances.

Some credit card users today have trouble staying out of debt. This trend may continue. Consumer education might help stop this problem.

Some consumers may continue buying the many things they want. Other consumers might begin to limit their spending. They might buy only the things they need. What do you think will happen?

◀ *A woman and her son use the computer to shop online with her credit card.*

Glossary

allowance—a sum of money given at regular times

budget—a plan for spending money to make sure that expenses are not bigger than income

charity—a group for donating money or help to those who need it

consumers—people who buy goods or services

credit cards—plastic cards that people can use as money that a bank has loaned them

debit cards—plastic cards that people use to take out money from their own bank accounts

debt—the money, time, or help that is owed to someone

donate—to give money, things, or time to help others

electronic money—money that is saved or spent by recording these changes in computer files

expenses—the money someone pays for needed or wanted goods and services

gamble—to bet money on who will win a game or race; also, to play a game for money

income—the money someone earns or gets

interest—the money a bank charges people for making loans to them; also, the extra money a bank adds to its depositors' accounts

loan—money given to someone that must be paid back

taxes—money collected and used by a government

Did You Know?

- One out of three high school seniors has already used a credit card.
- A man in California has the world's largest collection of credit cards. He keeps 1,356 cards in a wallet weighing 37 pounds!
- The Susan B. Anthony dollar coin never became popular. Because it was the size of a quarter, people had problems spending this dollar!

Want to Know More?

At the Library

Godfrey, Neale S. *Ultimate Kids' Money Book.* New York: Simon & Schuster, 1998.

Kyte, Kathy S. *The Kids' Complete Guide to Money.* New York: Alfred A. Knopf, 1984.

Otfinoski, Steve. *The Kid's Guide to Money: Earning It, Saving It, Spending It, Growing It, Sharing It.* New York: Scholastic, 1996.

Schwartz, David. M. *If You Made a Million.* New York: Lothrop, Lee, & Shepard, 1989.

On the Web

For more information about spending money, use FactHound to track down Web sites related to this book.

1. Go to *www.facthound.com*
2. Type in a search word related to this book or this book ID: 0756504856.
3. Click on the *Fetch It* button.

Your trusty FactHound will fetch the best Web sites for you!

Through the Mail

Bureau of Consumer Protection
Federal Trade Commission
600 Pennsylvania Ave. N.W.
Washington, DC 20580
To complain about unfair advertising or warranty problems

On the Road

American Advertising Museum
211 N.W. Fifth Ave.
Portland, OR 97209
503/226-0000
To learn about the history of advertising in America; open Wednesday through Saturday afternoons

William F. Eisner Museum of Advertising & Design at the Milwaukee Institute of Art & Design
208 N. Water St.
Milwaukee, WI 53202
414/847-3290
To learn more about advertising around the world; open Wednesday through Sunday afternoons

Index

About the Author

Natalie M. Rosinsky writes about economics, history, science, and other fun things. One of her two cats usually sits on her computer as she works in Mankato, Minnesota. Both cats enjoy pushing coins off tables and playing with dollar bills. Natalie earned graduate degrees from the University of Wisconsin and has been a high school and college teacher.